Musings from a Part-Time Mermaid

Kate Barker

BookLeaf Publishing

India | USA | UK

Presentation by *BookLeaf Publishing*

Web: www.bookleafpub.com

E-mail: info@bookleafpub.com

ISBN : 9789357448390

First edition 2021

DEDICATION

In dedication to Len Colville: the best Pop-Pop a young mer could have. He introduced Coochiemudlo to the family and in the process found 'my' place.

And to my husband, who has reached a point of resigned acceptance and will kayak while his wife mermaids.

The Song

There is a song that I hear with my feet;
Bare and pressed to the earth.
There is a thrumming in my bones
My soul vibrates with words I do not
understand,
In a language I do not know.
There is a language written on my skin,
Join the dots
               connect the freckles
                       trace the path

my family has taken.
See the journey across roiling waters,
Tossed to and fro on a wooden ship,
Praying that each storm would carry them
southward,
Rather than downward.
Leaving behind them a land of rolling, heather
clad hills,
Violet haze across distant mountains…
My Scottish story is written on my skin
And no one is surprised,
Looking at my hair, looking at my eyes,
When I feign to speak with a slight Scottish burr.
The bones in the family cupboard,
Have been dress-up'd in plaid,

Beribboned with dried lavender
Bones bleached white with age,
As white as the language of my skin
But bones I do not recognise save for the fact
that they, too,
Thrum with the song I hear with my feet.
Bones that are my core,
My foundation,
Unknown
And unnamed…
Because I do not have the words for
Bones that dance with salt-laden winds even as
my feet feel the song of the earth.
Scattered to those winds, dispersed among the
foam that floats atop ocean swells.
Self-arms stretch from a land of heat, wattle and
wingless dragons,
Over the ocean,
Past a land of soft violet and fresh cut grass on a
rainy day,
Returning to the land with a language I do not
know
But whose song I hear with my feet.
And in the thrum,
In the unknown
And the unnamed,
When fingertips meet
I find my
          self.

In Memory of Joy Fritz

I met her first in the garden
Argued with her in absentia
About the placement of the African Tulip
"it's a noxious weed" I said
"it's the sun in flower form" she said
"and what about this rope?"
I kicked the mud-stained coils
Pulled from the garden
Tossed another rusted spoke onto the
ever-growing pile
"did you follow the spirals around the sun in a
flowing fairy dance?"
She shook her head at my lack of romance
While I bemoaned the labour of artistry
trumping garden sense.

Next we met in the bay window
The desk became a seat
As I leaned against the window pane
Curled my fingers around a coffee mug
Watched the steam slowly slide into
The almost silence

While rain painted the day grey.
She sat opposite me.
Used the desk as a seat while she leaned against
the window pane
Captured melancholic beauty with her lens
While I fought to capture the sky with my pen.
My cat sat between us
Looked inside me
And purred at our reflections in the window.

We met in the ensuite;
Steam fogged the mirror
Blurred my senses as heat soaked my bones
Crystal balls formed along the ceiling
As we contemplated the teal feature wall
"what was I thinking?"
I shook my head, she was obviously thinking
something artistic
"that, you can change."
I didn't bother to point out that the house is mine
Instead, she sat with me while I planted ferns
Trained vines to grow along the edges
Coaxed flowers to bloom next to the bathroom
sink
Together we eyed the mural with critical eyes
Agreed that artistry had met functionality.

She was with me again in the garden
Sandy soil covered in sawdust

Watched me clear the space where the tulip had
been
Kept her sun circle
Filled it with sandstone seating surrounding a
blazing sun
She watched my children lie on the sandstone
Count the stars
Munch on toasted marshmallows
And her approval wrapped around my shoulders
Crocheted warmth during the winter nights.

I found her in her poetry
Trapped between the pages of a book gifted to
me
From one who knew her,
Before.
Toured our home through rhyming verse
And unreliable meter
Recognised our island in the photos
Illustrating poetry written in our garden
Looked up from the page and wondered
If the curlew nesting at the bottom of my stairs
Is a grandchild
Or great grandchild
Of the curlew that nested at the bottom of her
stairs.

When we met at Morwong
She stripped me bare

Coaxed me beneath the waters
Let the sun shine unabashed on bodies
Textured
Painted with natural night filtering through the
diamonds
Bobbing atop the ocean ripples
I showed her my mermaid self
Fearless in the blue
Showed her things her caution had kept hidden
from her
Like the muddies under the rocks
And the stingrays that glide along
The sandy floor
As the mermaid undulates along the water's
surface.

Some mornings she joins me
For coffee
As I lean on the verandah, eyes reaching for the
glimpse
Of blue
Between the trees
Some days she joins me for a swim
Explores the mangroves from oceanside
Night times are noisy
Busy with a young family
And she bemoans the peace and quiet
Even as her reflection in the window hides a
smile.

She joins me less and less
Trusts me to care for our house
To keep it a home
That welcomes flights of fancy
With wide arms
And open heart.
She misses her African tulip and the sun circle
But the past will hold on to the past
While the present lives for the future
And our home is filled with love
And Joy.

Yura, Coochiemudlo Island

Welcome to Coochiemudlo Island
Where the low tide laps at mangrove
Roots and cottonwoods beckon climbers with
whispered "yura"
Where hidden in the foliage the curlew
Makes her nest, where low tide beach teems
with life
As soldier crabs burrow beneath the sand they
call home.

Where high on the Telstra tower the Kite makes
her home
Where the ferry is the lifeline between mainland
and island
Where the wetlands bustle with life
Where the walking trail winds through
mangrove
And brush, where the curlew
Calls, heralding change with mournful "yura"

Where the Quandamooka offer "yura"
To those who now call Coochie home

Where the peacock socialises with the curlew
Fans his tail and parades the island
Where mudcrabs scuttle through mangroves
As they filter silt and bring the foreshore back to
life.

Where the bruised and bleeding find life
Hear the breeze over red cliffs murmur "yura"
Leave footprints on tidal sands, pick mangrove
Flowers from the waves, carry them home
Where they bring part of the island
Inside while in the garden nests the curlew.

Where the night-quiet is broken by curlew
Call, grieving loss from change, greeting new
life
As seasons cycle, almost unnoticed by the island
Healed, some leave; pass newcomers on the jetty
say "yura"
To those who come to call the island home
If only for the time it takes to walk the
mangroves.

Where the health of the island is measured in
mangrove
Wealth and the doleful call of the curlew
Where red mud stains the foundations of home,
Where native bees dance from flower to flower
bringing life

Where the mopoke and the kookaburra call
"Yura,
Welcome to Coochiemudlo Island."

Lessons from my Lovers

My body is a blank slate;
No piercings,
No ink,
No permanent billboard announcing: "this is
me"
My soul-self is Wagner's canvas—
A mosaic'd guestbook
Of all who have touched me,
And their touch tattoos upon my soul.
Some tattoos are pretty memories,
Some in memorandum,
And some are lessons from my lovers.

1.
My dating life started in year seven.
Hormones and social anxiety bubbled away
In a dangerous combination
That made me accept the first boy who asked.
We were twelve.
He was twenty.
We were school mates;

Not too sure what to do with the label of
boyfriend/girlfriend,
Tentatively holding hands beneath the desk
And my heart would race when simple skinship
Made his palms sweaty.
Not in love,
But in love with the idea of love.
He was a mentor,
Listened with sincerity,
Watched me bloom,
And when Mr 12 pinned his happiness
To a target on my back,
Shot barbed arrows blaming me
For unreciprocated affection,
Mr 20 taught me,
Love is not an obligation.
I don't think he expected me
To learn that lesson as well as I did,
When I walked away,
His gaze became the bullseye
Of the target tattooed between my shoulder
blades.

2.
We danced beneath the heavy summer moon
While cicadas hummed a waltz.
His hands were warm and dry
Pressing gently on the small of my back.
He picked a rose from the garden,

Offered me his admiration with a twirl
That made me join the stars in laughter,
And with moonlight in his eyes,
He saw past the past,
Taught me the joy
Of the dip and sway of a partner dance.
When summer faded,
A velvet petal bloomed between the dimples on
my back.

3.
We were going to get married.
High school sweethearts, I gave him my heart,
And my body.
Together, we explored the amazon of adulthood,
Played, unfettered in our adolescence,
Racing through the jungle
Then diving into the tempestuous Pacific of
love,
Sliding into salty sensuality
That slipped and slid over sensitive skin,
Only to collapse in a panting heap where the
forest meets the sea.
We were in love,
And his kisses planted jungle vines
That furled around my breasts.
Curling,
Ravenously growing,
Becoming the perfect camouflage

For the anaconda that called them home;
Squeezing my future into the desired shape
Until the day came that a tropical storm crossed
my coast,
Swept the snake away in flood water
And left the vines a crumpled reminder of how
he taught me
That a love that seeks to squeeze the jungle vine
Onto the domestic trellis
Is no love at all.

4.
The night we met,
Is the night we parted.
In the pungent heat of the club,
Strobe lighting turned the dancing crowd
Into a myriad of gyrating silhouettes;
Powered by the bass booming through our bones
The kelpie cavorted with the pooka,
The merrow taunted the Dullahoon,
And we connected on the dance floor—
Chest to back,
Butt to groin
And it was only thanks to the music that we
could call it dancing.
He put his hands on my hips,
Asked if he could touch me,
Asked if he could kiss me,
Listened to my words,

Not to what he thought my body was saying.
When his hands brushed my breasts,
They covered the dead vines with Scathach's
plaid,
As he swore fealty to the sovereignty of my
body,
Took a knee to the power of my "no."

5.
He was 'just for fun'
A summer fling who left tyre tracks
Tattooed on my thighs,
Targa-top cruising from foreshore to hinterland
Caressing the curves of the road stretched before
us
And we drove off into the sunset
Realised that if you keep driving west
The sun never sets
And the tyre marks became a golden ring
Circling the globe
Gravitating towards his sun.
One of these days,
I'll write my love a poem he doesn't need to
share
With anyone.

6.
Hail poetry
Capricious muse who taunts my lips

With feather kisses,
Trails a quill down my cheek as words
Spill forth to follow the faintest path.
She is warrior
Mother
Goddess
Temptress
Promises sweet release,
Cataclysmic bliss,
Leaves me gasping for air,
For more,
For her.
I call her master,
Grovel at her feet
Blank page offered in supplication
Pen poised to obey her every command….
Each pen stroke on the page bleeds lashes on my back
And my poems are inked with blood down the curve of my throat.

7.
I have learned to value my love,
To hold it as a priceless treasure that increases with worth
The more it is shared,
And sincerely returned.
I have learned that this body is not a land of exile

And my sovereignty is incontestable.
I have learned the toxicity of a love that corrodes
the self,
And the bliss of a love that sees the whole
And loves regardless.
And the day is coming,
When my soul-self will display a new tattoo—
A phoenix,
Rising from an amethyst heart,
Whose wings will drip fire down my arms,
And in that moment,
I will know that I have—
Finally—
Learned the greatest love lesson of all:
How to love myself.

Dear Daughter

When I was pregnant with my first,
I henna'd my belly
And stood barefoot in a rainforest stream.
A lone hiker passing by,
Stopped,
Looked at me standing there,
And said "you are an earth goddess dream,
Brought to life."
His words weighed upon my mind,
Unsettled me for years;
Was I only earthen goddess,
Gravid? And a wife?
This body has done so much more
Than carry a new babe,
Or kneel before the marital throne.
My worth is more than a ring of gold,
Heavier than a womb
Swelling with newly created life.
I am more than this.
We, are more than this.
More than the embodiment of servile maternity,
Chained to man.
Man would tell us,
Our body is a temple,

But oh, these words I say—
To more than me and mine—
Make no mistake, I speak to all the daughters,
Of all the mothers,
Whose breath has rippled through the ages of
time.
To all who have been,
Who will be,
And will spill upon the earth
Their blood, and sweat, and tears.
To you, I say;
Dear Daughter,
The rhythm of the ages is in your blood,
The thrum of the earth in your bones.
Your heart-song is a hymn eternal,
And you do not sing alone.
Before the temple ever was,
Was you,
Dear Daughter,
Cradled in that sacred water:
At peace, secure and calm.
Not fully formed yet infinite you reach
Through time and space; transcending flesh.
Three generations share a living heartbeat
And flicker as one.
Dear Daughter,
To celebrate your birth,
They will build you a temple
Of your own flesh.

With metaphor for marble
And condescension for mortar
They will cage your soul
In an altar of gold
And call it life.
In the freshly glowing dawn,
With the ardour of youth,
They will call you Rhea;
Dreaded goddess of Crete.
Your fierceness will be celebrated,
Engraved on bronze shields
And shouted from the battlefield.
They will call you Volcanic Pele.
She who's power, passion, and capriciousness
Are accessories for her beauty.
Both a lesson that a beautiful temper
Is seductive
For a face has power.
And men, young and old
Will come to worship at your temple
And their feet leave dirt on the marble
For no temple is ever fully free
From the builders.
Dear Daughter,
In your maturity,
Your temple walls will proclaim you
Primordial Gaia, wide bosomed mother earth,
Or fleet-footed Danu,
She who runs with streams o'er fields.

Maternal goddesses,
Whose incense is prayers for fertility.
Oh, Dear Daughter,
 Remember,
The rhythm of the ages is in your blood,
The thrum of the earth in your bones.
Your heart-song is a hymn eternal,
And you do not sing alone.
Dear Daughter,
When the sun is at its zenith,
Your name will fade in the afternoon haze.
Be whipped from your lips
By the wind
Before a single sound can slip free,
In your namelessness,
They will forget you.
Visit your temple no more
Until its presence becomes a threat
To a new world order.
Dear Daughter,
The world will batter at your door,
Rattle and shake your walls,
Demand entrance while your soul
Claims sanctuary.
Ancient lore of wealth and beauty,
Will lure the enemy.
The crusaders will come.
They will circle around,
Lay siege to your temple,

In the name of conformity,
In the guise of society,
They will bombard you
With unattainable expectations,
Loaded into catapults and
Aimed at your weakest point.
They will not miss,
For they built your temple
According to their own design.
They will topple your arches,
Fill the air with gunpowder
And the dust of shattered marble,
And declare themselves victorious
When you are reduced to a remnant
Of a by-gone age
For they do not understand;
That the rhythm of the ages is in your blood,
The thrum of the earth in your bones.
Your heart-song is a hymn eternal,
And you do not sing alone.
Dear Daughter,
Your temple is no sanctuary.
Do not let its ruins become your prison.
Instead, lay dormant for a moment,
Breathe with the forest that slowly grows around
you.
Inhale the richness of damp earth
And composting leaves,
Exhale the final specks of construction dust

Clogging your lungs.
Let the serenity of the rainforest
Seep beneath your skin,
Salve your soul with unspoken peace.
While you laze in the tranquillity,
Let the light filtering through the canopy
Bathe your skin with a golden sheen,
And turn your gaze inward.
Who are you?
Your crystal core flickers with a light
Fed by an internal source;
A light-spring welling from the earth,
Bubbling along the limpid stream murmuring in
your veins.
Dear Daughter,
In your temple,
You have forgotten your song;
A vague tune haunts your memory,
Purses your lips to hum,
But the words escape your grasp.
So wander the rainforest,
Bare-feet pressed against damp earth,
Ripples of a shared vibration in your bones,
Each step releasing the dark scent of life,
That springs from death.
Draw closer to your core,
Fill your lungs with free air,
Embrace your soul-self
And find your song once more.

Ignore the rowdy tourists
Who tread, uncaring, on your subducted tessera,
Graffiti their story onto marble
That has long lost its shine;
Let your namelessness,
Set you free.
Dear Daughter,
Give your temple to the forest;
Let the wompoo fruit dove nest in your eaves,
And paint your roof with fig seeds.
Let the pademelon shelter from the storm
Beneath a buckled pew,
And track fertile mud over broken floors.
Let the sun set on a desolate temple,
Embraced by carranoia vine and watkins fig,
Echoing with expectations
Made hollow by your absence.
You are a goddess,
Not because of your temple,
But because the rhythm of the ages,
Is in your blood;
Because the thrum of the earth,
Is in your bones;
Because your heart-song is a hymn eternal,
And you do not sing alone.

When I was pregnant with my first,
I henna'd my belly,
 And stood barefoot in a rainforest stream.

The rhythm of the ages was in my blood,
The thrum of the earth in my bones.
My heart-song was a hymn eternal
And we do not sing alone.

Pop Pop

He was old in my earliest memories:
Sun creased and weather worn,
Eyes the faded blue of summer sky
That dons a heat haze veil.
Flannel shirts hung on bony shoulders,
Grey whisps tucked under the felt fishing hat,
His present clouded with cataracts
But the past as sharp as ever.
With a great grandkid on each knee
He taught the alphabet backwards,
When to fish for flathead,
And the fisherman's greatest skill:
Untangling the trickiest of knots
In a loved one's heart.

Eulogy for the
Performance Poet

I was at a poetry slam when I heard you'd died
Thought the ear that thrilled to alliteration
And lyrical cadence
Had misheard.
Disrespected the poet on stage
And opened my phone.
Facebook wears so much make-up it's hard to
discern the lies
But maybe this time the truth would be
bare-faced,
Maybe this time the truth was a lie,
Maybe this time your absence
Was for personal growth
Or a social media break

And maybe it would be easy to say I never knew
you
But who knows you better than the people who
dissect you?
Who watch you stand on stage
Watch the microphone prise open your ribs
Watch your words leak from your beating heart

Watch liquid lyric pour from your veins,
Watch your tongue perform Seppuku
Spill yourself across the audience…

When we stand on stage,
We autopsy ourselves:
Offer our insides to the world to judge.
Each breath into the microphone is courage
Bravery
Is complete and utter vulnerability
We open ourselves to the audience
Put our shame in the spotlight,
Put our fear in the spotlight
Put our hopes and dreams and desires in the
spotlight
Put ourselves in the spotlight
No shadows to hide that which we want hidden
No shadows save for those we cast with the
spotlight,
No shadows save for those we paint with
words…

I was at a poetry slam when I heard you'd died
Wished I'd known you better,
Wished I'd known you not at all.
Wished I'd never seen what was inside…
Wished for half your courage as I readied myself
for my own vivisection.

I was at a poetry slam when I heard you'd died,
I was at a poetry slam...

29

Tidal Moon

The man in the moon sits above the window sill;
Silent smile speaks the words we cannot hear;
High C floats on the evening breeze,
Ebbs and flows with each inhale;
Feathers down the spines of those who sit in
darkness,
Lean towards the heart warmth glowing on the
verandah;
Community-heart throbs in tune,
Breath caught in unfeigned harmony;
Beneath the song that fills the air, the frog's duet
No discordant tone but the natural compliment;
Smell of rain, wet leaves and ebony night
And the island raises their voice as one;
When the mermaid sings

The Dancing Sabre

… if but a dream…

High noon bleeds oppressive heat
And the Sabre feints at her mooring post;
Flirts with the dappled waves,
Tethered to weathered wood by rusty chains.

Dreams of dancing 'cross the bay,
Freed from duty fuelled heartache,
Sail charged with crisp breeze— unfettered,
joyful.
Rusted chain tugs: just a dream.

Midnight and the raging winds
Whistle through neglected fetters— Sabre
dreams;
Ocean-logged wood groans and bends,
Iron flakes float on agitated sea.

The storm passes, dawn arises
And the Sabre wakes to new-found freedom,
Dances with the wind and waves; unknowing
That the unseen chain remains.

The Curlews' Call

The curlew called in the dead of night,
Woke her from her slumber sweet;
Once awake in summer heat
She sat by the window and bathed in starlight.

To her memories of time gone by she turned her
sight
To memories of lush green, and towering
heights.
The curlew called in the dead of night
Interrupted memories savoured as a treat.

Interrupted memories of adventures that might
one day fade; leave traces incomplete
of laughter, sore limbs, and bittersweet
Joy. To save them, she did write
while the curlew called in the dead of night.

The Curse of The Billy Of Tea

There once was a ship that put to sea
The name of the ship was the Billy of Tea
But there's more to the story that I'll tell ye
Of what did come before.

A sailor met a maiden fair—
Their eyes did meet 'cross market square
Cupid's arrow flew through the air
Just like a tale of yore.

He was a weathered sailor boy
She a white-lace beauty coy,
Neither did with the other toy;
Their love grew more and more.

He left her with a promise
To return, and with a kiss
Upon her rosy lips he swore to miss
She who was left on shore.

The voyage was long and winds did blow
Each day to the pier she did go

In hopes to that a sail on the horizon would
show
Her heart, each day, it tore.

"He'll ne'er come back" her parents said
Plans to marry her well swimming in their head
"The boy is likely drowned and dead,
The sea's a lethal draw."

Into the night the maiden crept
Of reuniting with her love she dreamt
Into the life of a cabin boy she leapt…
Women on the sea are cursed by lore.

Each day she would scrub the deck,
Learned to curse when the seagull peck'd
Watched land diminish beyond mere speck
Until one day the captain swore…

"Thar she blows boys" he cried
White plume stark against blue sky he spied
A whale worthy of whalers pride
All hands to the deck and down on her they
bore.

Had our maiden not crept aboard
The Billy Of Tea may at anchor be moored
Instead at her the sea-curse roared
And the ship sails on forever more.

One day the Wellerman will come
Bring them sugar and tea and rum
One day, the tonguing will be done,
And they can take their leave… and go…

The Certainties of Life (I)

Truth was fair of face and form.
She was mother, daughter, sister,
And unlike the emperor of old,
Her cloth revealed none of herself—
Woven from moonbeams
Caught in the frost that lay
On spider's web
In the breath before dawn—
Hem embellished with silk
Drawn from the chrysalis heart
That fears the unknown
But welcomes change
As the pulse inside translucent veins—
Her cloth reflects our image back at us:
Clear:
Unwavering.

The Certainties of Life (II)

Death is patient; touches each life at their time,
Counts not the seconds,
But their breath.
Death is kind; cool relief from the heat of the
dying,
Causes not the dying,
Gives peace.
It is not enviable, or prideful.
Not the cause for jealousy, or boasting.
It is not rude; offers courtesy in absolute
equality.
Death is not self-seeking, is not angered, and
keeps no record of wrongs.
It comes to all,
In their own time.
Death does not delight in evil,
But walks hand in hand with Truth.

The Certainties of Life (III)

Truth and Death walked hand in hand,
Between the flower beds.
Heads tilted towards the other,
Deep in heartfelt communication…
And Taxes trailed behind.

Truth and Death spoke poetry,
Brought pain, and fear and grief.
Brought peace, and love, and pure relief,
Kept the scales balanced
Within each earthbound life…
And Taxes trailed behind.

Truth and Death were welcomed
—   Though not without the initial sting of
rejection—
They were present everywhere breath was
released into the air,
And everywhere it wasn't.
Truth and Death were inevitable…
And Taxes.

Sirenarchy

Sirens are pack hunters:
Herd their prey into deep waters:
Circle the party of people creating currents that tug
At pedalling legs:
Unseen danger beneath the water
Pull them under
One …
        …by…
            …one…

Sirens are solitary hunters:
Stalk the shoreline,
Or the boats bobbing on full-moon tides:
Croon a watery lullaby that lures the unsuspecting
Into the inky bay…
They barely make a splash,
Leave faint ripples on the surface.

Sirens are opportunistic hunters:
Hunger a faint whisper
But the young floating in a tube beyond parental reach can be wrapped
In seaweed

Anchored to reef rock
Stored for when the current runs cold.

Sirens are stealth hunters:
Use the diamonds bobbing on the water to blind
Unwary swimmers
Coax them deeper with the promise of
sand-dollar etchings
They've never shown anyone else before…

Sirens are aggressive mimics:
Frolic like mermaids for the gawking,
The pointing…
Smile with closed lips to hide
Triangular teeth:
The only visual difference between predator and
pod.

Sirens are hunters not easily classified
Except to say:
Sirens hunt like Men.

Mother Marina

In the beginning God made the world.
Where once there was dark then there was light.
Empty space was populated and molten earth
became fertile.
Fertile land burst open in an eruption of feathers,
fur and fins and in the middle of this cacophony
of birth man emerged from the clay.

This has become the pivotal moment of
mankind's theatre.

The breathless moment in which a curtain is
raised upon a single actor haloed by the
back-light and the witless audience applauds as,
simply by his presence,
their expectations are met.

As with the stage, this moment did not happen
without the toil of those left behind in darkness.
Forgotten through the pages of history… or
vilified.

I was there.
One of the forgotten.

And the events that happened towards the end of
Act 1, Sc 1, didn't necessarily happen the way
the play has been written.
History has long been written by the victor after
all.
Well, by the victor who can write.
Illiteracy is an automatic disqualification from
the race of subjugation and oppression.
If you cannot leave a record of your victory
behind then who is to say you even won?
Who will care?
And so, now I write.

A few millennia too late to change the accolades
that the original version received but I was busy
at the time and scorned it for a passing fad.
Never did I foresee the popularity that a single,
prehistoric sapien would have… and the strange
little 'fandoms'- modern language has such
quaint expressions- that sprung up turned in to
fully fledge cults with people screaming,
wailing, flagellating, in the darkness… thinking
that chronic self-destruction would lead to light.
You want light? Wait for morning and watch the
sunrise. Homo Sapiens have never been the
brightest species to walk this planet. Ha. A pun.

I think that may have been my first.

My brother and I have long had what could best
be described as a tempestuous relationship.
He of earth, with fire at his heart, is quick of
thought and even quicker of action.
Rearranging continents because their positioning
is displeasing to the eye in that particular
moment of time: calling forth fully formed
creatures without allowing them the proper time
to grow: wiping the slate clean with asteroids,
famine, fire and then regretting his decision
immediately.

I have watched human children explore my
shores, pressing their small hands in to the
refuse of granulated shells crushed beneath my
breath, and misshapen lumps which they proudly
press leaf flags on to.
Always they build where my breath, my
sweeping exhale, will wash over their creation
and always they scream, red hot and trembling,
into the sky as though through sheer volume
they can turn back time.
My brother is as these sand moulders.
Immersed, to the point of abstraction, in his own
creation, he has forgotten to watch my breath.
Self-satisfied to the point of delusion he has
forgotten that time is my ally;

has forgotten to notice that with each breath I
drag myself,
heavy and laden with life,
up his shores,
grinding his earth with my shells and toppling
stone monoliths with barely a thought.
 He has forgotten, and in my depths I allowed
him to.

 It was from my womb that life was born:
mans' placenta my primordial sludge,
Embryonic salt transfigured to flow through
veins more delicate
than the gentle flowers that caress my cheek as
my breath ripples their stems.

 The surface world tumbles as my body heaves,
clenching and contracting in continual, tidal,
labour.
It is a new world that I am bringing to life.
A future wiped as clean and smooth as the
powder white expanses after a full moon.
 Heart beats splutter then dissipate into the foam,
fragments bleach in the sun then grind to dust,
polished to a glimmer in the sun by the very
waves that broke them down.

It is in this glimmer that I will write my story.
 It is in this story that I will write a new act.

It is my turn to have my voice heard.
My turn to remind my brother who I am.
My turn to guide the actors and shine a spotlight
upon the stage of my choosing.
It is my name that will be whispered through the
ages, revered, feared, hated, loved….

I am mother marina, sister ocean, daughter of
the moon and this time is my time.
Read your future in the sands…

… weep if you must; twill be to no avail.

It's almost opening night.

I am Leviathan.

When a Mother is Born

Back and forwards across the floor
Softly humming, paces the raw mother.
No-one sees, behind the closed door,
How she dreams of a time that's other.

Dreams of a time, like a foreign shore,
When arms around her, with love, would
smother.
Back and forwards across the floor,
Softly humming, paces the raw mother.

Dreams of a village; when neighbour and
brother,
Sister and friend, shared held and old wives'
lore.
Lives in a time with one-ness at its core,
When the miracle of birth is seen as a bother—
Back and forwards, across the floor,
Softly humming, paces the raw mother.

write the mermaid

blank page is mermaid grotto

fresh parchment
unmarked by ink
is tidal sandbank
exposed to the moon

pristine
inviting

felt tip pen
loaded with words and feelings
is mangrove seed
engraving the mermaid heart

on water-smoothed sand

In the Quiet Hours

He lies alone in a white-washed room,
Closed lids belie his quiet contemplation of
time's
Fragility. From the corridor muted whispers
Ebb and flow then gradually fade
Away until all that is left is the vacuum of loss.
Closed lids leak silent tears. The hand of fate
was not fair

When it wove this life. A travelling fair
Jangled in to town last year and he was ushered
in to a darkened room
Where predictions of pain and loss
Were scoffed at. He claimed time
Would prove the old gypsy wrong and let her
words fade
From memory. They return now, whispers

Tickling at his mind; taunting, questioning,
whispering
His fate. When he meets the ferryman how will
he pay his fare?
In coin? In tears? In the memory of love before
it fades

In to the darkness completely; like he fades
away in his white room?
A clock on the wall ticks with ominous
monotony as time
Trickles by; grains of sand grinding the gloss

From a young life. He can feel it- feel the loss
Of health, the loss of life. He can feel his body
whispering
Its eulogy before its time.
Restrained by white sheets he rails against the
unfair,
The unjust, against his isolation in a room
That orates the conclusion of his story before
life fades.

Caged by flesh and bone his humanity starts to
fade,
All that is left is desperation. And loss
Of hope. He could search for courage but has no
room
Left in his heart for more than the faintest
whisper
Of light to glimmer and paint a picture fairer
Than any he has seen in his brightest time.

Family visit with empty words of comfort as his
time

Draws to a close. Day runs in to night and light
fades
From behind drawn blinds. Dusk belongs to
magic, to fairies
And to passing. Dusk gives no regard to the loss
Of day but welcomes the dark with the tend'rst
of whispers.
He sleeps, until absolute silence engulfs the
room.

Hope

From the stagnant pools
Of muddied words and morals
Ah! The Lotus blooms.

Pieris Rapae

The easterly blew the fluttering flotilla off
course;
Swept them from the trees of Minjerriba
Across the sparkling waters of the bay.

Small white wings danced on the breeze,
Helpless to change direction
Could concentrate only on staying airborne.

From the blue beneath a mermaid poked her
head;
Watched with wide eyes and awe
As the cloud of living petals floated past.

She stretched a hand out and laughed
With joy when the cloud alighted on salty
fingers
Cried when the water on her skin made their
wings heavy.

More petals fell around her as exhausted
The butterflies could fly no more,
These she cradled gently till their friends had
reached the shore.

Once beyond the sandy break the wind lost all
its power;
Into the wetlands the butterflies disappeared
As though their forced migration never
happened.

The mermaid wears the petals in her hair and
each spring,
When the easterly blows across the bay,
She returns to dance with the Pieris Rapae.